Materials

Plastic

Cassie Mayer

Heinemann Library
Chicago, Illinois

Customer Service 888-454-2279
Visit our website at www.heinemannraintree.com

Picture research: Tracy Cummins and Heather Mauldin
Designed by Joanna Hinton-Malivoire
Printed in the United States of America in Eau Claire, Wisconsin. 111314 008624RP

ISBN-13: 978-1-4329-1619-0 (hc)
ISBN-13: 978-1-4329-1628-2 (pb)

The Library of Congress has cataloged the first edition as follows:
Mayer, Cassie.
  Plastic / Cassie Mayer.
    p. cm. -- (Materials)
  Includes bibliographical references and index.
  ISBN 978-1-4329-1619-0 (hc) -- ISBN 978-1-4329-1628-2 (pb) 1. Plastics--Juvenile literature. I. Title.
TP1125.M39 2008
620.1'923--dc22
                        2008005579

Acknowledgments
The author and publisher are grateful to the following for permission to reproduce copyright material: ©Corbis pp. **4** Jillian Pond/istockphoto/Rubber, **12** (SYGM/ Vo Trung Dunga), **15** (David Pollack), **20**, **22B** (Schlegelmilch); ©Getty Images pp. **5** (Time Line Pictures/ Sergio Dorantes), **9** (George Diebold), **11**, **23T** (Darren McCollester); ©Heinemann Raintree pp. **7**, **14**, **16**, **17**, **18**, **19**, **21**, **22M**, **22T**, **23B** (David Rigg); ©Jupiter Images pp. **10**, **23M** (Creatas Images); ©The New York Times p. **13** (Redux/ Hans Rudolf Oeser); ©Shutterstock pp. **6** (Prism_68), **8** (TIMURA).

Cover image used with permission of ©Corbis (Perry Mastrovito). Back cover image used with permission of ©Shutterstock (Prism_68).

Every effort has been made to contact copyright holders of any material reproduced in this book. Any omissions will be rectified in subsequent printings if notice is given to the publisher.

Contents

What Is Plastic? 4

What Happens When Plastic
  Is Heated? 10

Recycling Plastic 14

How Do We Use Plastic? 18

Things Made of Plastic 22

Picture Glossary. 23

Content Vocabulary for Teachers . 23

Note to Parents and Teachers 24

What Is Plastic?

Plastic is made from oil.

Plastic is made by people.

Plastic can be strong.

Plastic can be light.

Plastic can be stiff.

Plastic can bend.

What Happens When Plastic Is Heated?

Plastic can be heated.

Plastic can become a liquid.

Plastic can become cool in the air.

Plastic can become a new shape.

Recycling Plastic

Plastic can be recycled.

Plastic can be used to make new plastic.

Plastic can be used to make big things.

Plastic can be used to make
small things.

How Do We Use Plastic?

Plastic can be used to make bottles.

Plastic can be used to make toys.

Plastic can be used to make race cars.

Plastic can be used to make
many things.

Things Made of Plastic

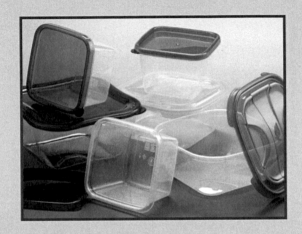

◄containers

▼race car

◄toy

Picture Glossary

 **liquid** flowing substance that has no shape.

 **melt** to change from a solid into a liquid. Some materials melt when heated.

 **recycle** to take old things and break them down. Then they are made into new things.

Content Vocabulary for Teachers

material Something that takes up space and can be used to make other things

Index

bottle, 18

liquid, 11

oil, 4

recycle, 14

toy, 19

Note to Parents and Teachers

Before reading

Show children a variety of objects made from plastic, such as a plastic bag, a clear plastic cup, a cellular phone, and any other diverse plastic objects. Ask children to sort the items into groups of color, texture, or use.

Give children an object made of plastic, such as a toy, and ask them to write down a list of descriptive words. Encourage them to think of the appearance, weight, feel, and use for the object.

After reading

- Ask children to look indoors for plastic objects that fit the following categories: strong, light, bendable, stiff, big, and small.